Old Friends, New Friends

written by Jenny Alexander
illustrated by Ken Stott

Chapter One

Nearly a Disaster

One Saturday the friends went up onto the common to ride their bikes. There were plenty of dirt tracks, which were fun to ride on.

The best one was through Tucker's Wood. It sloped downhill steadily for a couple of hundred metres, and then swerved sharply to the left. If they didn't get the speed just right, they would swerve off the path and end up in the bushes. They had all come a cropper there at some time, especially when the ground was muddy after a spell of rain.

The weather had been very windy for several days, and some twigs, broken off by the wind, were scattered across the path.

Everyone wanted the first go, so Jojo got four twigs and held them in one hand so that only the ends were showing.

"Choose a stick," she said. "The person who gets the shortest one can go first."

It was Ben.

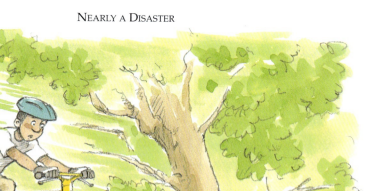

He shot down the hill on the dry bumpy path.

The trees on either side
were a blur of brown and green.
Suddenly, as he slowed down to take
the bend, he saw a movement in the bushes,
and a boy leaped out onto the track, yelling
and waving his arms about.

Ben slammed on the brakes, and came swerving
to a stop. The bike slid out from under him, and he
tumbled onto the path.

"What did you do that for?" he demanded angrily,
struggling to get up.

The boy was about the same age as Ben. He had long
brown hair, which he wore in tatty dreadlocks. Ben had
never seen him before. The boy had obviously been
running, and he was too out of breath to speak.
He walked down to the bend and pointed. There was
a broken branch blocking the path. If Ben had come
hurtling round the bend at top speed, it would have been
a disaster.

"I saw you at the top of the hill with your bikes,
so I took a short cut through the woods to warn you,"
the boy said, breathlessly.

"How did you know the branch was here?" Ben asked.
"I know everything that happens on the common.
I live here at the moment," said the boy. The boy grinned
and then, without another word, he strolled
off down the track.

When he had disappeared from sight, Ben gave himself
a shake. "I didn't thank him!" he exclaimed. "He saved
me from having a really bad accident." He heaved his
bike over the fallen branch, jumped on, and rode after
the boy. The others followed him.

But by the time they got to the edge of the wood,
the boy had gone.

"Where did he go?" said Sam.

Ben shrugged. "We've lost him," he said.

"We can find him again, though," Jojo said. "He's on
foot, and we've got bikes. We can cover the whole area
really fast."

"Let's go!" agreed the others.

Chapter Two

Travellers

The friends searched for the boy for ages, but they couldn't find him. Eventually, they gave up and cycled back towards the road, to see if there was an ice cream van in the Cut.

The Cut was a large lay-by on the narrow road that ran through the middle of the common. There wasn't an ice cream van, only an old bus parked at the far end, with a line of washing running from one window to the **'DO NOT LEAVE LITTER'** sign.

"Travellers," Sam said.

"We'd better leave it," said Mouse, uneasily.

Jojo agreed. "We can't hang around here," she said. "It looks odd."

But Ben still wanted to say thank you. He had only gone a few steps when a big dog came out, with its head low to the ground. It growled at him. He stopped in his tracks. He couldn't go on, but he didn't want to turn his back on the dog. The dog started barking, and Ben took a step backwards.

Straight away, the boy from the woods came out of the bus. He walked over to the dog. "It's okay, Prince," he said, taking hold of its collar. The dog stopped barking, but it didn't take its eyes off Ben.

"You saved me from having a nasty accident," Ben told the boy. "I just wanted to say thank you."

The boy smiled. His teeth looked bright white in his sun-tanned face. He didn't say anything.

"Now you've saved me from that dog, as well," said Ben.

The boy said, "He wouldn't have hurt you. Not so long as you stayed away from the bus, anyway."

Ben swallowed. He had been planning to knock on the door. "Do you live in the bus?" he asked the boy. The boy nodded. They both stood looking at the bus.

"Have you always lived in it?" asked Ben. The boy nodded again. There was an awkward silence. "My mum hasn't, though," said the boy. "She was born and brought up in the town. That's why we're here, to see my gran and grandpa."

The boy let go of the dog, and it went right up to Ben and sniffed his legs. It would have tickled him if he hadn't felt so scared. "Is it just you and your mum?" Ben asked. He hoped that if he kept talking, the dog would see he wanted to be friends.

8

The boy said that for a lot of the time it was just the two of them. But sometimes they had friends travelling in the bus, especially if they were doing a big catering job. That was how they earned their living, providing hot food at festivals. They had a trailer full of catering equipment that they left in a lorry park between jobs.

To Ben's relief, the dog stopped sniffing him and went to lie in the shade under the bus.

"Do you want to have a look inside?" asked the boy. There was nothing Ben would have liked more. However, he knew he shouldn't even talk to strangers, let alone get into their buses.

"I'd better not," he said. But he didn't want to go. He was still curious about the boy, and he liked him.

At the top of the Cut, the others were getting restless. They couldn't hear what Ben and the boy were talking about, but they were shy of going to join in.

Ben asked the boy, "Have you got electricity?" The boy shook his head.

"So – no television?" Ben exclaimed. "No computers!"

He looked so horrified, the boy burst out laughing.

A woman came out of the bus, and emptied some dirty water into the ditch. "Who's this, Jack?" she asked, coming over.

"A friend."

"Ben," said Ben.

"Hello, Ben," said the woman.

She seemed really nice, and Ben was sure it would be all right for him to go into the bus, but he knew he ought to check with his parents first. "I've got to go now," he said. "We're supposed to be home before lunchtime."

Jack said, "Come back this afternoon if you like."

Ben nodded. As he got back on his bike and cycled up to the road with his friends, it occurred to him that life might be quite lonely for a traveller like Jack.

Chapter Three

Shouldn't, Mustn't, Can't

When Ben told his parents at lunch time about his near-accident in the woods, they were shocked.

"You shouldn't be riding your bike down steep slopes with sharp bends," said his father. When he told them about going to find the boy so he could say thank you, his mother said, "You mustn't talk to strangers."

When he asked if he could go back that afternoon and see what the bus was like inside, both his parents said no.

"You can't go calling on people you don't know," they said.

Ben wasn't going to give up without a fight. "You let me go to Donut's house when he first came, and I didn't know him. What's the difference?"

"He only lives down the road," said Ben's mother.

"And he goes to your school," added his father.

Tessa was helping herself to peas. "That's the real problem, isn't it?" she said. "This boy hasn't got a house and he doesn't go to school. You're just being narrow-minded about people who have a different lifestyle."

Her parents exchanged a look.

"I mean, what's wrong with travellers?" Tessa went on. "Just because they don't live the same way as we do doesn't mean they're bad, does it? As a matter of fact, living in a bus is very good for the environment. If more people did it, we'd have less global warming."

Ben pushed his food around the plate with his fork. He couldn't believe his parents were being so unreasonable. "It's all 'shouldn't, mustn't, can't,'" he grumbled. "What *can* I do, then?"

His mum sighed. "If you're so keen to get to know this boy," she said, "you can ask him over here. He can come for tea."

Ben could hardly wait to go back to the common.

When he got to the Cut, he found Jack sitting on the grass, stroking Prince.

"I was wondering if you'd like to come to my house? You could stay for tea," Ben said.

"Okay," said Jack. "I'll just ask Mum."

Jack went into the bus, and the dog sat looking at Ben. It was an uncomfortable couple of minutes. Then Jack came back out with his mum. She talked to Ben for a while, and asked him questions. Ben could tell she was trying to make up her mind about him. "And you're sure your mum and dad are happy about you having Jack over to play?" she said.

Ben nodded. "Mum's doing baked potatoes for tea."

14

Jack's mum said he could go to Ben's house, but she wanted to take him there in the bus so that she knew where he was, and fetch him back later.

"You can put your bike in the bus," said Jack. "There's a huge storage space underneath." His mum started taking in the washing and untying the line. Jack opened the door of the storage space.

"My mum says I can't go inside your bus," said Ben.

The two boys frowned at each other. Then they laughed.

"That's great, isn't it?" said Jack. "Your mum won't let you go in the bus, and my mum won't let me not go in the bus!"

"What are we going to do?" said Ben.

Chapter Four

What's Going On?

Ben went ahead on his bike to show the way, and Jack and his mum followed in the bus. They made very slow progress into Story Street. People on the pavement turned to stare as they went by, and a long tailback of cars soon began to build up behind them.

In the flats, Sam heard a lot of shouting and tooting of horns, and she went outside to see what was blocking the traffic. She bumped into Donut. "What's going on?" she said.

He shrugged. "That's what I'd like to know," he told her.

They walked up to the bend in the road, and then they
saw the old bus pulling up outside Ben's house. Ben
appeared on the pavement, riding his bike. Sam and
Donut went to investigate.

The rumble of the bus's engine and the hiss of its brakes
brought Mouse and Jojo to their window in the house next
door.

"It's that boy's bus!" Jojo exclaimed.

"What's going on?" asked Mouse.

"There's only one way to find out," said Jojo, pulling
on her shoes.

Mouse and Jojo, Sam and Donut all arrived on the pavement outside Ben's house at the same time. Ben told them Jack was coming to play. Jack jumped down from the bus. He seemed delighted to see everyone.

"What time shall I come back for you?" his mum asked. She didn't appear to have noticed that she was causing a major traffic jam. She told Ben, "Perhaps I should have a quick word with your mother."

At that very moment, Anna King came hurtling through the park gates dressed in her running gear. She almost ploughed straight into them.

"This is my friend Jack." Ben told his mum. "And this is his bus."

Mrs King stared at the huge old bus in astonishment. Inside, Jack's mum leaned across the steering wheel to say hello and to ask Mrs King what time she should come back for him. Mrs King said, "About seven o'clock would be ..."

Suddenly, Anna King stopped. She moved closer. She peered into the bus. "Sarah?" she said.

Jack's mum came out from behind the wheel. She jumped down onto the pavement. "Anna!" she exclaimed.

The two women stood in the middle of the pavement, staring at each other. A traffic warden arrived. "You cannot park that vehicle on the public highway," he said. He took out his ticket book.

Mrs King told Jack's mum where the nearest car park was. "Come back and have some tea with us when you've parked the bus," she said. "We've got an awful lot of catching up to do!"

Jack's mum got back in the bus and started the engine. It rumbled and shook like a washing machine full of trainers.

"What's going on?" Ben asked Jack.

Jack shrugged.

As the bus disappeared into Bridge Street, Mrs King told them she had been in the same class as Jack's mum in the local secondary school years ago. She looked as if she might start talking about the old days, and Ben knew from experience that once she got going they would never get away. So he asked Jack quickly if he liked computer games.

"Ben's got loads of them!" Mouse exclaimed.

"We could have a tournament," suggested Donut.

Mrs King was leaning on the fence, waiting for Jack's mum to come back. "I would steer clear of your father," she said to Ben, not turning around. "His computer's crashed and he thinks he's lost some files."

Ben nodded, and they all made for the door.

Chapter Five

Old Friends, New Friends

The two mums sat in the garden drinking tea and talking about the old days.

Ben played with his old friends and his new friend in his room. It felt like a birthday party because there were so many of them. They were all happy and excited to have someone different around for a change.

Mrs King was in a party mood too. She invited everyone to stay for tea. She baked plenty of potatoes, and Jack's mum helped her to prepare lots of salads. They all sat down to eat, except Mr King who was upstairs, locked in combat with his computer.

"Do you enjoy travelling around?" Mrs King asked. "Doesn't it get a bit lonely?"

Jack told her he had lots of friends. They were always getting together with other travellers, or joining in with protests about new roads, runways and green site development. There were music festivals and fairs to go to and, several times a year, they came to see his grandparents in Story Street.

"Now, I can come and see Ben as well," he said.

Jack and his mum had lots of stories about living on the bus. They made everybody laugh.

"But seriously, Sarah," Ben's mum said, in a moment of quiet. "What I can't understand is how you came to live on a bus in the first place. I mean, I was good at sports, and I became a fitness instructor. You were good at everything else, and you ended up living on a bus. It doesn't make sense."

"Well, I went to university," Jack's mum explained, "and that was okay. After that, I got a job in London, and that was okay. But I got very homesick, so I came back here quite often at weekends. Then, one day I came back to find they were digging up Bluebell Wood to build a new road."

The shock of seeing the countryside she had known all her life becoming spoiled made Jack's mum feel terribly sad. She didn't want to be part of a society that seemed to value concrete above animals and grass.

"So you gave up everything to do what you believed in?" said Anna King, in amazement. "You gave up washing machines, microwaves, television ..."

"CD players,"
added Tessa. "Personal stereos ..."
  "Computers," said Ben.
  There was a crash from
Mr King's office, and
a loud yell.

Jack's mum said she didn't pine for the things she had given up because of all the things she had gained.
They looked at each other. What on earth could she mean?
    "Have you ever watched the sun rise?" she asked them.
    "I've seen it speeded up on Nature Today," said Jojo.
    "I've seen pictures of it," added Mouse.
    "But have you ever actually seen it in real life?"
said Jack.

They all shook their heads. Even Mrs King had never seen it.

"I've lived for nearly forty years, and I've never watched the sun rise," she said. "Isn't that odd?"

Jack said, "I know! Let's go over to Hartman Hill tonight and watch the sun rise together."

Mrs King started to gather the empty plates. "Oh, I don't know …" she said. She opened the freezer to look for some ice cream.

"Go on!" pleaded Ben. "It's Sunday tomorrow."

"We can ask our mum," said Mouse. "She's bound to let us if you let Ben."

"So's mine," said Donut.

"And mine," said Sam. "Oh, can we, Mrs King?"

Mrs King said, "Well …"

Before she could stop them, Mouse and Jojo raced off to ask their mum, and Sam and Donut went to ask theirs.

"You haven't had any ... pudding," Mrs King called after them, looking down at the tub of toffee ice cream in her hand.

"I'm still here!" said Jack, with a grin.

Tessa got some bowls out of the cupboard and gave them to her mum. "I almost wish I wasn't going to the disco now," she said.

Mrs King served up the ice cream. She was wondering how she had managed to let things go so far. "We'd better finish our tea and find some warm clothes if we're going to spend half the night sitting on a chilly hilltop," she said.

Chapter Six

On Hartman Hill

It was dark by the time Jack's mum brought the old bus back round to the house. The friends were waiting eagerly with their spare sweaters and sleeping bags. They climbed up into the bus. There were two rows of seats in the front. The back of the bus was screened off by a thick, heavy curtain.

They drove across the common and through the housing estates at the edge of the town. They came out towards the ring road. Then they took the main road south.

Far off in the distance, they could see the black mass of Hartman Hill silhouetted against the sky.

The bus couldn't go very fast. It chugged along in the slow lane and then turned into the maze of narrow lanes that criss-crossed the fields at the bottom of the hill. They parked in an old quarry.

Jack pulled back the curtain and they followed him into the back of the bus. He turned on the light. They found themselves in a living room with white painted walls and brightly-coloured hangings. There were rugs and cushions on the floor. On one side, there was a wood-burning stove, and on the other side a long, soft sofa. There were shelves with bars across, to stop things falling off.

"Where do you sleep?" asked Jojo.

The back of the bus was separated from the living area by a partition wall. Jack opened the door, and showed them his bedroom. The bed was high up on a wide shelf, and there were cupboards underneath. One of them was full of books. Mouse was surprised.

"Can you read?" he said.

Jack laughed. "You don't have to go to school to learn to read," he said.

As well as Jack's room, there was a tiny bathroom and a second bedroom at the back of the bus. They went back to the living area. Jack's mum had lit the wood-burner, and it was starting to feel quite cosy. She made some hot chocolate. Then they got into their sleeping bags and settled down on the floor for a few hours' sleep.

Ben didn't realise he had been asleep until his mum woke him up. It was time to go up the hill. Everyone put on their thick sweaters and went outside. It was very dark. There was no moon, but the sky was full of stars. They had never seen so many stars. Some were big, and twinkled fiercely, others were tiny white dots, clustered together like a milky dusting across the top of the sky.

"You don't see many stars in the town," Jack said. "There's too much light pollution."

When their eyes got used to the darkness, they could see the path by starlight alone. They could hear small creatures moving in the bracken. Jack led the way, with the friends next and the two women at the back with the dog. It was a long climb.

At the top it was cold and breezy, but there was a wind shelter made of rocks and stones. They huddled together to wait. They talked quietly in the darkness about all sorts of things. Then they all fell silent. Ben looked at his watch. It was twenty past five.

There was a great feeling of expectation. After a few moments, the silence was broken by a burst of birdsong in the dark. Other birds gave an answering call. Then suddenly, pale yellow light spilled up over the horizon, and the sun, like a yellow, misty jewel, drifted up into the sky. It happened as they watched – they could actually see it rising. The landscape came out of the darkness, and the world woke up.

"That was incredible!" they said.

The sunshine sparkled on the dewy grass as they went back down to the bus for breakfast.

"We could be staying near Hartman Hill soon," Jack told them. "A property developer wants to build a huge shopping centre here. There's going to be a big protest."

"I could come out and see you," said Ben.

"You could all come. You could meet some of my other friends," said Jack.

They looked at each other, doubtfully. "Your other friends aren't like us," they said.

Jack laughed. "You liked seeing the sun rise on Hartman Hill, didn't you?"

They nodded.

"Then my other friends are just like you!" he said.